GRANDMA AND GRANDPA'S TRAVELING HOUSE

A TRAVELING SARFF'S ADVENTURE

THIS BOOK BELONGS TO:

____

FOR ALL THE GRANDCHILDREN
WITH TRAVELING GRANDPARENTS
AND THE ADVENTURES THEY SHARE
TOGETHER

JACK, MORGAN AND LITTLE LAINEY ARE COUSINS. THEY LOVE TO PLAY TOGETHER AND SHARE ADVENTURES.

THEIR GRANDPARENTS ARE FULL-TIME RV TRAVELERS. EVEN THOUGH THEY MISS SEEING THEM EVERY DAY, THEY LOVE HEARING ABOUT THE NEW PLACES THEY VISIT AND THEIR ADVENTURES ACROSS THE USA.

DO NOT OPEN
DO NOT OPEN
DO NOT OPEN

EACH DAY, THE CHILDREN CHECK THEIR MAILBOXES TO SEE IF THEIR GRANDPARENTS SENT THEM ANYTHING FROM THE LATEST STATE THEY ARE VISITING.

THIS WEEK, THEY EACH RECEIVED A LARGE BOX WITH "DO NOT OPEN" STAMPED ON IT. WHERE COULD GRANDMA T AND GRANDPA DAVE BE THIS WEEK AND WHAT COULD BE IN THE BOX?

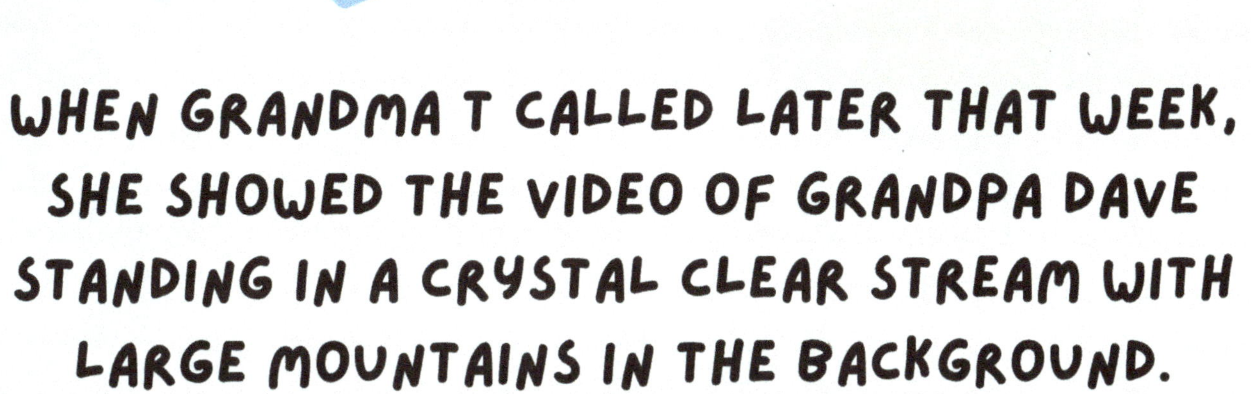

WHEN GRANDMA T CALLED LATER THAT WEEK, SHE SHOWED THE VIDEO OF GRANDPA DAVE STANDING IN A CRYSTAL CLEAR STREAM WITH LARGE MOUNTAINS IN THE BACKGROUND.

"WELCOME TO MONTANA," SAID GRANDMA T. "GRANDPA DAVE IS TRYING TO CATCH SOME TROUT FOR OUR DINNER IN ONE OF THE MANY STREAMS THAT FILL WITH WATER FROM SNOWMELT IN THE MOUNTAINS."

JACK LAUGHED. "I SEE FISH JUMPING BUT GRANDPA DAVE DOESN'T SEEM TO HAVE ANY LUCK CATCHING THEM!"

MORGAN GASPED. "WHAT BEAUTIFUL MOUNTAINS. SO MANY COLORS AND THE WATER LOOKS SO CLEAR!"

LITTLE LAINEY JUST DROOLED HAPPILY.

LAUGHING, GRANDMA T AND GRANDPA DAVE MADE THEIR WAY TO THE BANK NEXT TO THE STREAM. "BREAK TIME," SAID GRANDMA T.

AS THEY SAT DOWN TO CHAT WITH THE CHILDREN, A PRETTY BIRD LANDED IN A TREE.

"LOOK," SHE SAID. "IT'S A WESTERN MEADOWLARK. THAT'S THE MONTANA STATE BIRD."

MONTANA

"MONTANA WAS ONE OF THE LATER STATES TO JOIN THE USA," SAID GRANDPA DAVE. "THE CAPITAL IS HELENA, AND IT BECAME OUR 41ST STATE IN 1889."

"LONG AGO, TWO EXPLORERS NAMED LEWIS AND CLARK TRAVELED WEST ACROSS THE PLAINS TO THIS MOUNTAINOUS AREA. THEY WERE MAKING MAPS SO PEOPLE WOULD KNOW WHAT WAS HERE."

"I PICTURE THEM CROSSING THE FLAT GROUND OF THE PLAINS AND THEN SEEING THE HUGE ROCKY MOUNTAINS RISING UP FROM THE GROUND IN THE DISTANCE. WHAT A SIGHT THAT MUST HAVE BEEN," SAID GRANDMA T.

"THAT SOUNDS SO COOL," SAID JACK. "I WONDER IF THEY CAUGHT ANY FISH?" HE GIGGLED.

GRANDPA DAVE LAUGHED, "IT'S STILL ONE OF OUR WILDEST STATES. IT'S FULL OF NATURE, ANIMALS, RIVERS AND STREAMS."

"DID YOU KNOW MONTANA HAS MORE GRIZZLY BEARS THAN ANY OTHER STATE EXCEPT ALASKA? IMAGINE THE SURPRISE OF LEWIS AND CLARK WHEN THEY SAW THOSE FOR THE FIRST TIME!" SAID GRANDPA DAVE.

"I LOVE BEARS," SAID MORGAN. "I BET THEY WERE CUTE."

"CUTE BUT DANGEROUS," HE REPLIED.

"ONCE THIS AREA WAS MAPPED, WAGON TRAINS STARTED MAKING THEIR WAY HERE. THEY WERE FULL OF MEN AND FAMILIES THAT WANTED TO BUILD A NEW LIFE."

"WAGON TRAINS?" ASKED JACK. "WHAT'S THAT?"

"A WAGON TRAIN IS A GROUP OF COVERED WAGONS THAT WERE PULLED BY TEAMS OF ANIMALS. THEY HELD ALL A FAMILY'S FOOD AND TOOLS AND OTHER THINGS THEY WOULD NEED TO BUILD THEIR NEW HOMES."

"THAT SOUNDS LIKE YOUR CAMPER," SAID JACK.

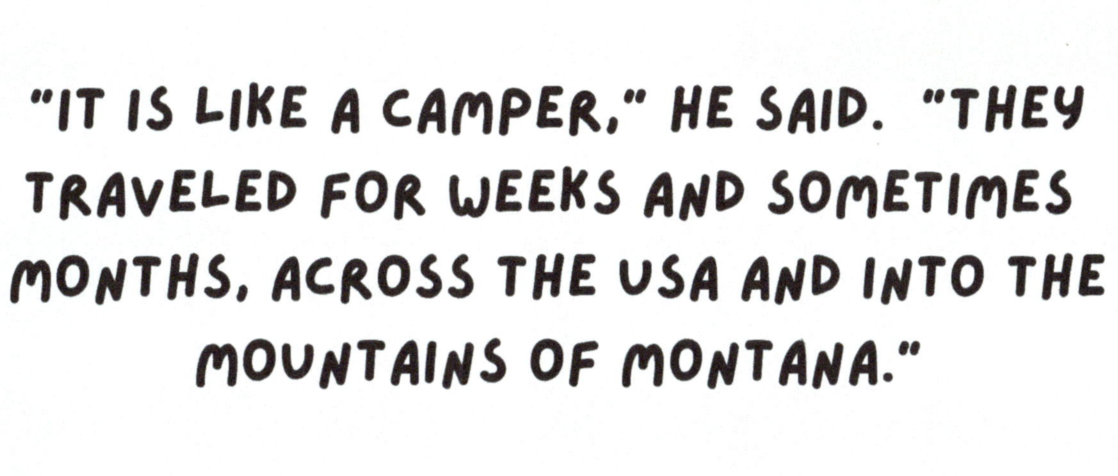

"IT IS LIKE A CAMPER," HE SAID. "THEY TRAVELED FOR WEEKS AND SOMETIMES MONTHS, ACROSS THE USA AND INTO THE MOUNTAINS OF MONTANA."

"IMAGINE SEEING ANIMALS LIKE BIGHORN SHEEP GRAZING IN THE VALLEYS OF THE MOUNTAINS AND WILD BITTERROOT GROWING ACROSS THE PLAINS AS YOU TRAVEL. IN FACT, BITTERROOT IS THE STATE FLOWER," HE FINISHED.

"EVERYDAY WOULD BE SOMETHING NEW TO SEE,"
SAID MORGAN. "THAT SOUNDS AMAZING!"

"DID THEY SLEEP IN THE WAGONS?" ASKED JACK.
"THAT SOUNDS LIKE FUN TO ME!"

"THEY DID," SAID GRANDMA T. "THE WAGONS
WOULD ALL GATHER IN A CIRCLE EACH EVENING
TO KEEP EVERYONE SAFE DURING THE NIGHT."

"MEN WOULD STAY UP AND KEEP WATCH OVER THE PEOPLE WHILE THEY SLEPT. IT WAS SO DARK AT NIGHT, AND THE STARS WERE SO BRIGHT, IT SEEMED YOU COULD SEE FOR MILES AND MILES. THAT'S WHY MONTANA IS KNOWN AS BIG SKY COUNTRY."

"THAT SOUNDS BEAUTIFUL," SAID MORGAN. "I'D LIKE TO SEE THOSE STARS SOMEDAY."

GOLD!
MONT
186

"AS THE PEOPLE STARTED TO BUILD THEIR NEW HOMES, SOME OF THEM FOUND GOLD IN THE RIVERS, CREEKS AND MOUNTAINS. THIS CAUSED MORE AND MORE PEOPLE TO HEAD THIS WAY AND BEFORE YOU KNEW IT, MONTANA HAD BECOME PART OF THE WILD WEST."

"WHAT'S THAT?" ASKED JACK. "LIKE COWBOYS AND RODEOS?"

ON
GOLD!

"SOME WERE COWBOYS," CONTINUED GRANDPA DAVE. "THERE WERE ALSO SHOPKEEPERS, FARMERS, AND PEOPLE LOOKING FOR GOLD WHO WANTED TO GET RICH."

"THEY CALLED IT THE WILD WEST BECAUSE IT GREW VERY FAST. TOWNS WOULD START ALMOST OVERNIGHT, AND THERE WERE VERY FEW LAWMEN TO KEEP THE PEACE. IT COULD BE QUITE 'WILD' AND DANGEROUS AT TIMES."

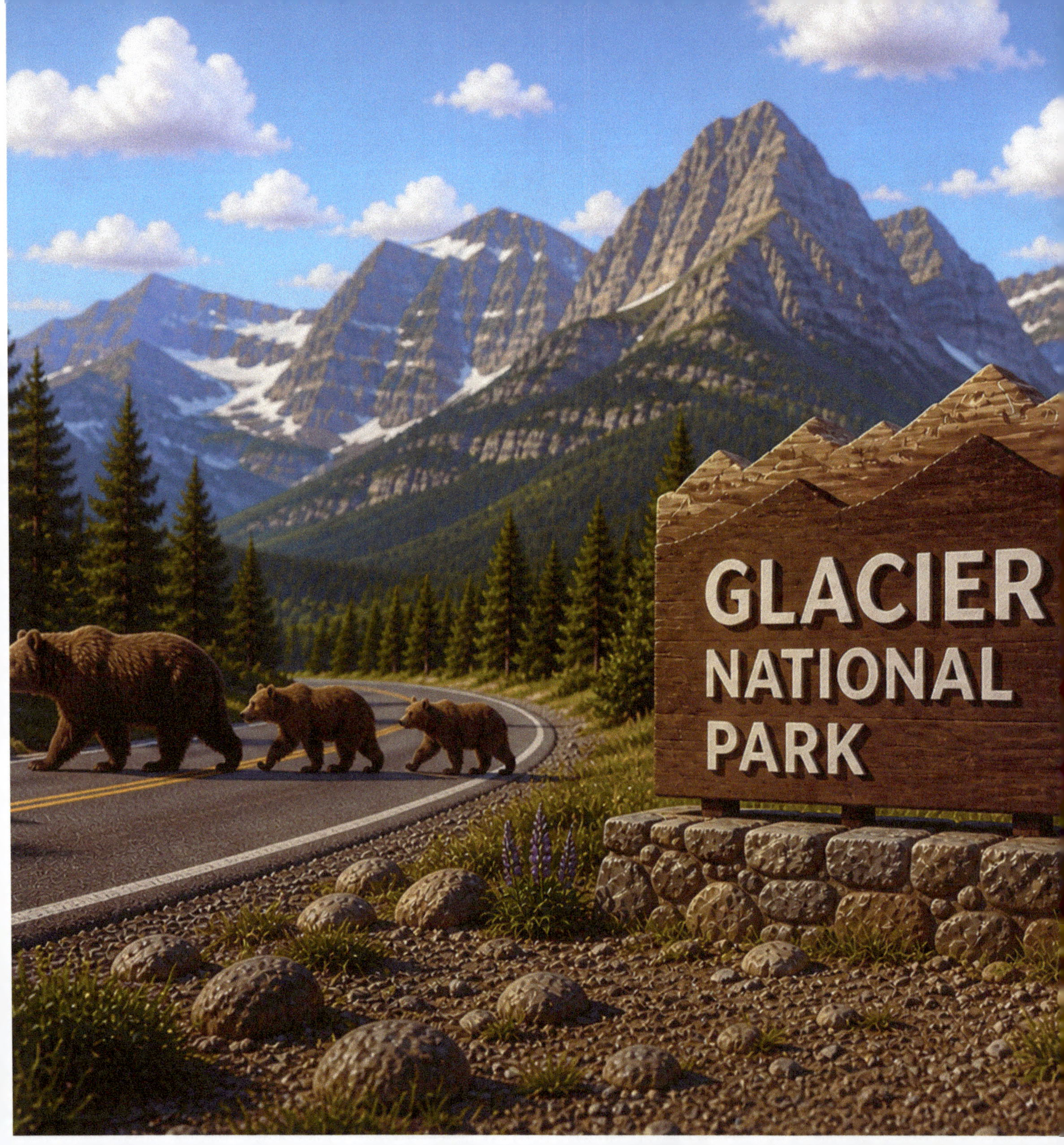

GLACIER
NATIONAL
PARK

"AFTER IT SETTLED DOWN IN THE LATE 1800s, ANOTHER EXPLORER NAMED GEORGE GRINNELL WANTED TO PROTECT PARTS OF THIS BEAUTIFUL STATE. HE WANTED TO MAKE SURE THE MOUNTAINS AND RIVERS AND STREAMS WERE SAVED SO EVERYONE COULD VISIT THEM. IN 1910, GLACIER NATIONAL PARK WAS CREATED FOR THAT VERY REASON."

"WHY IS IT CALLED GLACIER NATIONAL PARK?" ASKED JACK.

"GLACIERS ARE BIG CHUNKS OF ICE THAT MOVED ACROSS THIS LAND. LONG AGO, THEY PUSHED THEIR WAY THROUGH THE MOUNTAINS AND CREATED GREAT VALLEYS. THERE ARE STILL SOME GLACIERS HERE TODAY."

"I LOVE THAT," SAID MORGAN. "THAT MEANS WHEN I GET OLD ENOUGH, I CAN VISIT AND SEE THEM FOR MYSELF."

"I WANT TO CAMP IN IT," SAID JACK. "IN A COVERED WAGON!"

GRANDMA T AND GRANDPA DAVE LAUGHED.

"TODAY, MONTANA IS STILL FULL OF WILD ANIMALS, BUT THERE ARE ALSO LOTS OF CATTLE RANCHES. MONTANA NOW HAS MORE COWS THAN PEOPLE," SAID GRANDPA DAVE.

"MORE COWS AND MORE GRIZZLY BEARS THAN PEOPLE," SAID JACK. "THAT IS A LOT OF ANIMALS."

AS THE CHILDREN WATCHED, GRANDPA DAVE WENT BACK INTO THE STREAM TO START FISHING AGAIN. THEY TALKED ABOUT SCHOOL AND ALL THE FUN THINGS THE CHILDREN WERE DOING AROUND THEIR OWN HOMES.

SUDDENLY, GRANDPA DAVE HAD A BIG JERK ON HIS FISHING POLE AND PULLED OUT A FAT TROUT.

"YEAH!" THE CHILDREN CHEERED.

"FINALLY!" SAID GRANDPA DAVE. "THAT WAS A FIGHTER FOR SURE!"

GRABBING HIS FISH AND GATHERING THEIR PICNIC SUPPLIES, GRANDMA T AND GRANDPA DAVE WALKED BACK TOWARD THEIR CAMPER. ON THEIR WAY, THEY ALL SPOTTED A SMALL FAMILY OF BADGERS ON THE SIDE OF THE TRAIL.

"MONTANA SURE HAS A LOT OF ANIMALS," SAID MORGAN. "THIS MIGHT BE MY FAVORITE STATE SO FAR."

"IT'S DEFINITELY ONE OF OUR FAVORITES," SAID GRANDMA T. "IT FEELS JUST LIKE WE ARE BACK IN TIME AND EXPLORING MONTANA FOR OURSELVES."

WATCHING THROUGH THE SCREEN WITH A LAST LOOK TOWARD THE SKY, LITTLE LAINEY KICKED THE CARDBOARD BOX IN FRONT OF HER.

GRANDPA DAVE LAUGHED. "IT'S TIME TO OPEN YOUR BOXES," HE SAID.

THE CHILDREN MADE QUICK WORK OF GETTING
THEM OPEN AND ALL SHOUTED WITH SURPRISE AT
THE GIANT STUFFED GRIZZLY BEARS THEY HAD
RECEIVED.

"MOST GRIZZLIES OUTSIDE OF ALASKA," SAID
JACK. "I'LL ALWAYS REMEMBER THAT NOW!"

MORGAN HUGGED HER BEAR TIGHT AND LITTLE
LAINEY DROOLED ON HERS. SILLY LAINEY!

AS THE FISH FINISHED COOKING, IT WAS TIME FOR GRANDMA T AND GRANDPA DAVE TO END THE CALL.

"WE LOVE AND MISS YOU," THEY SAID. "WE'LL TALK AGAIN SOON."

"WE LOVE AND MISS YOU TOO," SAID JACK AND MORGAN WHILE LITTLE LAINEY WAVED HAPPILY.

THAT NIGHT AS THE CHILDREN SLEPT HOLDING
THEIR NEW BEARS IN THEIR ARMS, THEY DREAMED
OF MONTANA AND ALL THEY HAD SEEN.

IT ALMOST FELT LIKE THE BEARS WERE GIVING
THEM GIANT GRANDMA T AND GRANDPA DAVE
BEAR HUGS, AND THOSE WERE THE BEST!

MONTANA WAS A BEAUTIFUL AND SPECIAL PLACE
AND THEY COULDN'T WAIT TO SEE IT SOMEDAY.

UNITED STATES OF AMERICA
PACIFIC OCEAN
WASHINGTON
OREGON
MONTANA
NORTH DAKOTA
MINNESOTA
WISCONSIN
MICHIGAN
NEW YORK
MAINE
IDAHO
SOUTH DAKOTA
LAS VEGAS
WELCOME TO FABULOUS LAS VEGAS NEVADA
WYOMING
NEBRASKA
IOWA
ILLINOIS
INDIANA
OHIO
PENNSYLVANIA
MARYLAND
CALIFORNIA
NEVADA
UTAH
COLORADO
KANSAS
MISSOURI
KENTUCKY
WEST VIRGINIA
VIRGINIA
HOLLYWOOD
NEW MEXICO
OKLAHOMA
ARKANSAS
TENNESSEE
NORTH CAROLINA
SOUTH CAROLINA
ARIZONA
Route 66
MISSISSIPPI
ALABAMA
GEORGIA
LOUISIANA
FLORIDA
TEXAS
GULF OF MEXICO
ALASKA
HAWAII
ATLANTIC OCEAN
N W E S

Enjoy Grandma and Grandpa's Traveling House?
Ready to see where they go next?

Join their adventures as they travel through each U.S. state and share what they've learned with their grandkids—Jack, Morgan, and Little Lainey.

Each book includes a postcard from the state traveled. Collect them all and add them to your own Grandma and Grandpa's Traveling House postcard album.

Grandma and Grandpa's Postcard Album

Cut along dotted line and add to
The Traveling House Postcard Album

THIS PAGE LEFT INTENTIONALLY BLANK